REMEMBER REMEMBER

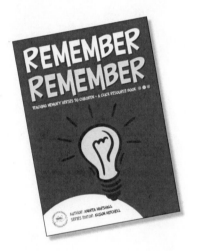

TEACHING MEMORY VERSES TO CHILDREN

Author: Andrea Marshall

Series Editor: Alison Mitchell

thegoodbook
COMPANY

Remember Remember: Teaching memory verses to children
© The Good Book Company 2008
Printed 2008, reprinted 2012, 2016, 2017

Published by The Good Book Company, Blenheim House, 1 Blenheim Road, Epsom, Surrey, KT19 9AP, UK.
Tel: 0333 123 0880; International: +44 (0) 208 942 0880
Email: admin@thegoodbook.co.uk

Websites:
UK: www.thegoodbook.co.uk
North America: www.thegoodbook.com
Australia: www.thegoodbook.com.au
New Zealand: www.thegoodbook.co.nz

Original material written by Andrea Marshall. Edited by Alison Mitchell (alison@thegoodbook.co.uk).

ISBN: 978-1-905564-75-0

Designs by Wild Associates Ltd and Jon Bradley. Extra illustrations by Kirsty McAllister.
Printed in the United Kingdom.

REMEMBER REMEMBER
TEACHING MEMORY VERSES TO CHILDREN

CONTENTS

WHY REMEMBER?

Notes for leaders

Learning a memory verse is a regular part of most children's sessions—but why do we do this, and what is the long-term value of memorising Bible verses?

This chapter looks at these questions and then considers some of the practical issues we need to bear in mind when teaching God's living Word to children.

But as for you, continue in what you have learned and have become convinced of, because you know those from whom you learned it, and how from infancy you have known the holy Scriptures, which are able to make you wise for salvation through faith in Christ Jesus. 2 Timothy 3 v 14–15 (NIV)

Notes for leaders

Why remember?

In the passage above, Paul reminds Timothy that he knew the Bible from infancy—and that the Scriptures he was taught "are able to make you wise for salvation through faith in Christ Jesus" (**2 Timothy 3 v 15**). The Bible is God's living Word. Through it, He reveals Himself to us and shows us how we are to live as His rescued people. Through God's Word, we meet the risen Jesus and come to understand who He is and why He came. It's no wonder that teaching the Bible, as faithfully and effectively as we can, is at the heart of the work we do with children!

Memorising Scripture is something believers have done for thousands of years: "These commandments that I give you today are to be upon your hearts" **Deuteronomy 6 v 6**; "I have hidden your word in my heart that I might not sin against you" **Psalm 119 v 11**. As we teach memory verses to children, we are helping a new generation to hide God's Word in their hearts as well, so that they can get to know God better and understand how He wants them to live for Him. This is why we must be careful to teach the meaning of a verse as well as helping children memorise the words.

In the book of Deuteronomy, we find a pattern of daily life for believers: "Fix these words of mine in your hearts and minds ... Teach them to your children, talking about them when you sit at home and when you walk along the road, when you lie down and when you get up" (**Deuteronomy 11 v 18–19**).

God's Word is at the centre of this pattern—but how often do we actually have a copy of the Bible in our pocket while sitting at home, walking along the road and so on? Sometimes, maybe—but not always. But if we have "fixed God's words in our hearts and minds", then they are always with us.

This command is primarily for parents. They are the ones who have the responsibility for the spiritual education of their children. Our role as children's leaders is to be in partnership with parents, supporting them in teaching Christian truth to their children. One way we can do that is by helping children to learn God's words for themselves. Those words will then be with them when they walk and talk with their parents (Christian or not)—and also when they walk and talk with their friends. One great reason for Christian children to memorise God's Word is so that they can then tell their friends what God says, and point them to the joy of knowing Jesus.

What to remember

Do your children ever check up on you? Do they simply accept all that you tell them about God, or do they ask how you know? When we work with children, especially younger ones, we need to be careful about how we teach them. A young child will tend to accept everything we say uncritically—which means we must be careful not to abuse that trust. But if a child is going to put their faith in Jesus, and grow in their relationship with God, it's vital that this growth is built on God's own Word, not merely on what what their leaders say.

When Paul visited the city of Berea, he told the people the fantastic news about Jesus. The Bereans were thrilled—but they also checked up on Paul! "They received the message with great eagerness and examined the Scriptures every day to see if what Paul said was true" (**Acts 17 v 11**). We want the children we teach to do the same—to find out for themselves what God's Word says.

This may be a good reason to collect together a number of memory verses to teach your group—verses that sum up key Christian truth. John 3 v 16 would be a good place to start! Then plan to teach these verses during your year, even if they don't appear in whichever teaching material you are following at the time. This way, the children can be sure the vital things they are learning about God's character, and why He sent Jesus, really do come from God's own Word.

You may also want to consider learning a larger section of Scripture with the children. Typically, memory verses tend to be short, and may change every week or so. But most children are quite capable of learning more. One group of 7-11 year-olds learned the whole of Philippians 2 v 1-11 during a term of teaching about the character of Jesus. We learned a little bit at a time, building it up gradually, and using actions to help us. By the end of term, every child (and their leaders!) could remember the entire section.

How to remember

In this book you will find 96 different ideas for teaching memory verses to children. Here are a few practical points to bear in mind as you try out those ideas, and choose which ones will be most suitable for your group.

Choose your verse carefully

In many cases, a memory verse will be suggested as part of any teaching material you use. Do check that this verse really does support the main teaching point of the passage. If it doesn't, replace it with something that will back up what you are teaching that day. If the suggested verse comes from another part of the Bible, look it up so that you can check the context and make sure it really is saying what you think.

Consider which Bible version to use

Whenever possible, teach verses from the same version the children will be looking them up in. If you have a set of Bibles you use with your group, then teach from this version. Alternatively, choose the version that children are most likely to have at home. Be consistent in teaching from the same version—and never hunt around through different versions until you find the one that happens to say what you want!

Decide whether to include the reference

A simple rule of thumb when teaching memory verses is that you include the Bible reference once children are able to look it up for themselves. Until then, the reference can be meaningless and confusing. So, a group of 3-5s will probably just learn that Jesus said: "I am the light of the world". But 5-7s and 7-11s would also learn that He said this in **John 8 v 12**.

Teach the meaning, not just the words

When you are teaching a memory verse, it is important that you check that the children understand its meaning. You may do this in the context of the story you are teaching, or at a separate time. Make sure that you explain any difficult words or concepts. Check the children's understanding by asking them to tell you what the verse means in their own words.

Use lower case lettering

When children are learning to read, they learn lower case letters first. These are much easier and quicker to recognise than capital letters. (This is why most road signs use lower case text.) When writing out a memory verse, write it clearly, and as large as possible, using lower case letters. If you use a computer to print your verse, rather than writing it by hand, try to choose a font that uses the kind of letter "a" that children write by hand. **Comic Sans** is an easily available font that includes this kind of "a". **Futura** and **Sassoon** are other good options if you have access to them.

Aim for good quality

We are teaching God's living Word—so if possible, avoid writing out memory verses on old, battered paper using pens that have almost run out! It is worth investing in good quality marker pens, and brightly coloured craft paper—and using a ruler. The result will be easier for children to read, as well as looking much better. Buying a low-cost metre ruler from a DIY shop will help you to write out long verses neatly, which will again be easier for the children to read.

Note: This book contains a number of photocopiable pages to help you prepare for the activities.
All of these photocopiables can also be downloaded for free from the following websites:

UK: www.thegoodbook.co.uk
North America: www.thegoodbook.com
Australia: www.thegoodbook.com.au
New Zealand: www.thegoodbook.co.nz

Be aware of learning styles

Much has been written about learning styles. However, a simple summary is that people learn in different ways. This applies to both adults and children. A simple summary would be:

- some children learn best by **listening** (auditory learning)
- some children learn best by **looking** (visual learning)
- some children learn best by **doing** (kinesthetic learning)

So, when you teach a memory verse, choose a number of different activities from this book so that children have the opportunity to learn in a variety of ways. This will give all of them the best opportunity to learn and remember God's Word.

BY THE BOARD

Notes for leaders

The games in this section only require the use of a black or white board, and a board rubber.

You may find it helpful, before trying any of the following activities, to read the practical tips on page 7. In particular, remember to use lower case letters when writing out a memory verse. Unless you are teaching very young children, who are not yet reading, you should include the Bible reference as well as the verse.

How sweet are your words to my taste, sweeter than honey to my mouth!
Psalm 119 v 103 (NIV)

By the board—contents

Voices

Age-range: 3–8 year-olds

Gear

▶ A black or white board
▶ Board rubber

Use this as an introduction to another activity or as an activity in its own right. Write out the memory verse on the board. (Alternatively, you could write the verse on cards or a large piece of paper.) Read through the memory verse in a variety of ways; for example: read it quickly or slowly; whisper or shout; use a squeaky voice, sing or, for older children, use a silly accent.

Squeak piggy squeak

Age-range: 3–8 year-olds

Gear

▶ A black or white board
▶ Board rubber

Seat the children in a group. Choose one child to come to the front and turn their back to the group. Point at one of the other children without saying their name. This child then recites the memory verse in a squeaky voice. The child at the front tries to guess who squeaked. Choose a different child to come to the front and repeat the process. As the game progresses, rub out words from the memory verse so that the children are saying more and more of the verse from memory.

Around the circle

Age-range: 3–8 year-olds

Gear

▶ A black or white board
▶ Board rubber

Seat the children in a circle on the floor, leaving enough room for the children to run around the outside of the circle safely. Choose one child to be the leader. As the rest of the children chant the memory verse, this child walks around the outside of the circle gently touching the seated children on the head, one touch for each word of the memory verse. The child who is touched as the last word is chanted chases the leader around the outside of the circle back to the empty place. The last child to sit down then becomes the leader and the game begins again.

Sign

Age-range: 3–11 year-olds

Gear

▶ A black or white board
▶ Board rubber

Use British Sign Language, Makaton or Sign Supported English to sign key words of the memory verse as you recite the memory verse together. This is particularly useful to support children with special educational needs, communication difficulties or a hearing impairment.

You may know a teacher or parent who can show you the signs you need. Alternatively, check the following websites for information: www.britishsignlanguage.com, www.makaton.org or for signs used in the Deaf Christian Community try www.christiansigns.co.uk

Grandmother's footsteps

Age-range: 5–7 year-olds

Gear

▶ A black or white board
▶ Board rubber

Display the memory verse on the board at the front of the room. The children line up along the back of the room, facing the board. Choose one child, the "Grandmother," to come to the front and face the wall next to the board. The aim of the game is to be the first person to reach the board without being seen by Grandmother. As the children move towards Grandmother, she turns round to try and catch them moving; the children try to stand still before she sees them. If the Grandmother sees any of the children move, they either recite the memory verse correctly or get sent back to the beginning. The first child to reach Grandmother takes her place and the game begins again.

Play the game several times so that most or all of the children get a chance to be Grandmother. Rub out words in the memory verse as the game progresses until the children are reciting the verse from memory.

Wipe-out

Age-range: 5–9 year-olds

Gear
▶ A black or white board
▶ Board rubber

Use this as an activity to introduce the memory verse. Write the memory verse and reference onto the board using a different colour to highlight key words and the reference. Recite the memory verse together two or three times. Ask one of the children to come to the front, choose a word to rub out and then point to the words while the memory verse is read through again. Continue choosing different children to rub out a word, reading the memory verse through together each time until there are no words left and the children are reciting the verse from memory.

All change

Age-range: 5–9 year-olds

Gear
▶ A black or white board
▶ Board rubber

Seat the children in a circle. The aim of the game is to say the memory verse as quickly as possible around this circle, each child saying a word in turn. Choose one child to start, and the direction of travel; then recite the memory verse one word at a time. When the children have finished reciting the memory verse, the leader calls out: "All change!" and the children swap places with each other. The leader then chooses another child to start reciting the memory verse and the game begins again. Continue playing until the children have swapped places four or five times.

Clap

Age-range: 5–9 year-olds

Gear
▶ A black or white board
▶ Board rubber

Write the memory verse on the board, highlighting the key words in a different colour. Recite the memory verse, then choose a child to rub out one of the words. Recite the memory verse together again, replacing the missing word with a clap. Continue rubbing out words and replacing them with a clap until all the words have been removed.

Clapman

Age-range: 5–9 year-olds

Gear
▶ A black or white board
▶ Board rubber

Write the memory verse on the board and read it together once or twice. Rub out the first word and recite the memory verse again, replacing the missing word with a clap. Continue rubbing out one word at a time, reciting the memory verse and replacing the missing word with a clap each time.

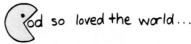

Alternatively, remove words in the reverse order…

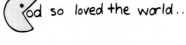

Alphabet clap

Age-range: 5–9 year-olds

Gear
▶ A black or white board
▶ Board rubber

Write the memory verse on the board and read it through together once or twice. Once the children are familiar with the memory verse, rub out all the words beginning with the letter "A". Recite the memory verse again, replacing the missing words with a clap. Continue to rub out words in alphabetical order until all the words have been removed and replaced with a clap.

A B C D E F G H I J K L M
N O P Q R S T U V W X Y Z

Number clap

Age-range: 5–9 year-olds

Gear
- A black or white board
- Board rubber

Write the memory verse on the board and read it through together two or three times. Rub out words in the order of their length, starting either with those containing the most letters or those with the least number of letters. Each time you remove words, read through the memory verse and replace the missing words with a clap.

Bus-stop

Age-range: 5–11 year-olds

Gear
- A black or white board
- Board rubber

Use the Bible story from your session in a memory verse game. Divide the children into equal teams. Seat the teams in parallel lines so that the teams are next to each other and the members of each team are one behind another, as on a bus. Leave spaces between the chairs of each team and between the teams so children can get in and out of their chair easily and safely.

Give children character names from the story, so that all the children at the front of their team have the same character, all the children second in line have the same character as each other, and so on back through the teams.

The children listen for their character's name as the adult tells the story. When they hear their character mentioned, they leave their seats to the left, run around the front and back of their team and return to their chair. (This should be on the same side as they left it.) The child who is the first back into their chair recites the memory verse and, if they are correct, they gain a point for their team. The adult continues the story while children continue to listen for their character. You may choose to display the memory verse, removing words as the game progresses.

Hangman

Age-range: 5–11 year-olds

Gear
- A black or white board
- Board rubber

This game works best when introducing the memory verse for the first time. As in the traditional game, draw out one dash for each letter of each word, separating the words with a slash (/). Either divide the children into teams or play as a whole group.

Children or teams take turns to choose a letter. If it is in the memory verse, fill in that letter in all the places that it occurs. If the letter does not appear in the memory verse, draw the next part of the hangman. You may choose to write the incorrect letter on the board to remind the children which letters have been chosen. When playing in teams, a point can be given to each team for guessing a letter in the verse or for each time that letter occurs. Alternatively, the winning team is the last team to survive the hangman or the first team to guess the memory verse correctly.

For a group with younger children, write out the alphabet and cross off the letters as they are chosen. Younger children who cannot remember letter names or sounds could choose a letter by pointing to the alphabet.

As an alternative to the hangman picture, other pictures may be drawn to link this game to your topic. For example, a boat, crown, pyramid, tree...

Ladders

Age-range: 5–11 year-olds

Gear

▶ A black or white board
▶ Board rubber

Divide the children into two equal teams. Form a ladder by seating the teams in two lines on the floor, each child facing a member of the other team. Children sit with their legs straight out in front of them, their feet touching those of the person opposite to form a pair or rung of the ladder. Number the pairs of children.

When the leader calls out a number, the pair of children with that number stand up, race down the middle of the ladder, stepping over the other children's legs, around the outside of their team and back down the ladder to their place. The child who is back first recites the memory verse and, if this is done correctly, they gain a point for their team. You may choose to display the memory verse, removing one word at a time as the game progresses.

Make sure that the children understand the importance of being careful when they step over the other children's legs. Don't play this game if you have children in your group who are likely to be careless or unsafe when stepping over each other.

Gold, silver, bronze

Age-range: 7–11 year-olds

Gear

▶ A black or white board
▶ Board rubber

Sit the children in a circle. Make a gap between the "beginning" and "end" of the circle. Label the three places nearest to the beginning of the circle as gold, silver, and bronze. The aim is to be the person sitting in the gold position at the end of the game.

The person in the gold seat starts the game by saying the first word of the memory verse, silver says the second, bronze the third and so on around the circle, continuing across the gap at the end if there are more words in the memory verse than children. If anyone makes a mistake or does not say their word quickly enough, they move to the last place in the circle, other children moving up to make room for them. The memory verse then starts again from the beginning. If no mistakes are made, continue reciting the memory verse around the circle without returning to the gold position. You may choose to display the memory verse on the board and remove words as the game progresses.

ON THE CARDS

Notes for leaders

All the games in this section require a set of memory-verse cards. Write the memory verse and reference onto cards so that there is one word on each card. Use lower case letters when writing out the memory verse (see page 7).

The games in Part One need only one set of cards. For those in Part Two, one set of cards per team is needed, each set of cards a different colour.

Heaven and earth will pass away, but my words will never pass away. Matthew 24 v 35 (NIV)

On the cards—contents

On the cards—Part One

The games in this first part need only one set of memory-verse cards.

Word sort

Age-range: 5–7 year-olds

Gear

- One set of memory-verse cards, with one word written on each card
- Blu-tac reuseable adhesive

This can be used as a quick introduction to another game or activity—for example, **Take away** (page 17). Mix up the memory-verse cards and stick these cards to a board or wall with Blu-tac. Ask one child to come and choose the first word of the memory verse and stick it to the left of the board. Choose another child to find the next word and so on. Continue finding the words in order until the whole memory verse has been assembled. Try to run through this activity fairly quickly to keep the children's interest. Read through the memory verse at the end.

When using this activity with older children, it can be made more challenging by reassembling the memory verse in reverse order, starting with the reference.

People sort

Age-range: 5–7 year-olds

Gear

- One set of memory-verse cards, with one word written on each card

Choose some children to come to the front, one for each word of the memory verse. Mix up the memory-verse cards and give the children at the front one card each. Ask one or two of the other children to sort the memory verse into the correct order by moving the children who are holding the cards. The children who are watching can help those doing the sorting by calling out instructions. Read through the memory verse together at the end to check that it is in the correct order. You may wish to play the game again to give children a turn in a different role.

Pop-up

Age-range: 5–7 year-olds

Gear

- One set of memory-verse cards, with one word written on each card. (Extra sets may be needed if you have a larger group.)

If you have a small number of children, sit them in a semicircle or line. Alternatively, seat the children with a little space around each child. Divide the cards among the children so that they all have at least one card. (Extra sets of the memory-verse cards may be required.)

When told to begin, the child or children with the first word "pops up" and shouts out the word on the card, followed by those with the second word, then the third and so on through the whole memory verse. Play again, challenging the children to be even quicker the second time through. You may choose to redistribute the cards among the children before playing again.

Zig-zag

Age-range: 5–7 year-olds

Gear

- One set of memory-verse cards, with one word written on each card
- Blu-tac reuseable adhesive

Stick the memory-verse cards around the room so that each successive word is as far away as possible from the preceding word. Start with the children in the centre of the room; then walk to each word of the memory verse in order, calling out the memory verse as you go. Repeat this by hopping, jumping, skipping, tiptoeing or crawling to the cards in turn, choosing the movement to suit the size and layout of your room.

Turn about

Age-range: 5–9 year-olds

Gear

▶ One set of memory-verse cards, with one word written on each card

Ask some children to come to the front and hold the memory-verse cards, showing the memory verse in the correct order. Read through the memory verse together several times before asking two or three of the children to turn around and face the other way. Ask those children not at the front to read through the verse, replacing the missing words. Call out: "Turn about!" The children holding the cards all turn around, each choosing to make either a full or half turn, thus displaying a different part of the memory verse for the children to read and fill in the missing words. Repeat several times. On the command: "All hide!", all the children holding a card face away from the group who then recite the verse from memory. You may choose to give other children a turn at the front.

If you are playing this game with a small number of children, arrange the children into a circle or semicircle and ask children to turn the card rather than themselves. This allows all the children to read through the memory verse.

Take away

Age-range: 5–9 year-olds

Gear

▶ One set of memory-verse cards, with one word written on each card
▶ Blu-tac reuseable adhesive

Stick the memory-verse cards in order to a board or wall. Recite the memory verse together two to three times before choosing one child to remove a card and point to the memory verse for everyone to read. Continue choosing different children until all the cards have been removed.

When all the cards have been removed, you may choose to play another game such as **Pop up** (page 16) or **Hang out the washing** (page 25).

Chain game

Age-range: 6–9 year-olds

Gear

▶ One set of memory-verse cards, with one word written on each card

This game requires at least as many children as there are words in the memory verse. Give out one card to each child and ask the children to spread out around the room. Children keep repeating the word that is on their card. The child with the first word walks around listening for the child with the second word. When found, they link arms, forming a chain. The child with second word then leads the chain, listening for the third word of the memory verse. Continue building the chain in this way, so that the most recent child to join is the one who leads the chain to find the next word.

If there are a few children who do not have a memory-verse card, they can make it more difficult for the children in the chain by shouting out silly words; for example: "bananas", "hairy caterpillars" or "smelly feet".

Circle sort

Age-range: 7–11 year-olds

Gear

▶ One set of memory-verse cards, with one word written on each card

Seat the children on chairs in a circle, with an extra empty chair somewhere within the circle. Give out a memory-verse card to each child so that the words of the memory verse are in a random order. The children have to sort themselves out into the correct order by moving around the circle. Children are only allowed to move to an adjacent empty chair or "jump" over one person at a time.

See **Hat game** (page 53) for a more challenging version of this game.

② On the cards—Part Two

The games in this second part need one set of memory-verse cards per team. Each set of cards should be a different colour. Read through the memory verse several times after each game.

Go find

Age-range: 5–9 year-olds

Gear

▶ One set of memory-verse cards per team, with one word written on each card. Each set needs to be a different colour.

Place the cards around the room in different locations; for example: under tables, on chairs or stuck to the wall. Vary the difficulty of the hiding places according to the age of the children. Divide the children into equal teams. One child in turn from each team searches for one word card to bring back to their team. When all the words have been found, the children rearrange the words into the correct order, with a little adult help if necessary. It is helpful if the leader and any helpers know how many cards need to be collected for each team.

Relay

Age-range: 5–9 year-olds

Gear

▶ One set of memory-verse cards per team, with one word written on each card. Each set needs to be a different colour.
▶ Blu-tac reuseable adhesive (optional)

Stick the memory-verse cards to a board or wall so that all the cards from all the teams are mixed together. Alternatively, arrange them on the floor or tables at one end of the room. Divide the children into equal teams and line them up one behind the other at the opposite side of the room. One child in turn from each team runs to collect one card for their team, bringing it back to a table or floor. When all the cards have been collected, the teams arrange the cards in the correct order. Read through the memory verse together once or twice.

As an alternative to running to collect the cards, the children can hop, jump or use their hands and feet to travel across the room.

Relay order

Age-range: 5–9 year-olds

Gear

▶ One set of memory-verse cards per team, with one word written on each card. Each set needs to be a different colour.

Arrange the memory-verse cards face up at one end of the room, so that all the cards from all the teams are mixed together. Divide the children into equal teams and line them up one behind the other at the opposite side of the room. One child in turn from each team runs to collect one card for their team. Cards must be collected in the order that they appear in the memory verse. You may choose to number the cards to help children order the words.

As an alternative to running to collect the cards, the children can hop, jump or use their hands and feet to travel across the room.

Order order

Age-range: 5–9 year-olds

Gear

▶ One set of memory-verse cards per team, with one word written on each card. Each set needs to be a different colour.

Place the memory-verse cards around the room in different locations; for example: under tables, on chairs or stuck to the wall. Vary the difficulty of the hiding places according to the age of the children. Divide the children into equal teams. The first child in each team searches for the first word of the memory verse and brings it back to the team; then the second child searches for the second word, and so on. Continue hunting the words in order until all have been found. The winning team is the first one to find the words in the correct order. If possible have an adult for each team or pair of teams checking that they find the words in order.

Under the table

Age-range: 5–9 year-olds

Gear

▶ Two sets of memory-verse cards, with one word written on each card. Each set needs to be a different colour.

▶ Table (or two tables, pushed together)

▶ Blu-tac reuseable adhesive (optional)

Hide the cards under the table—on the floor, stuck to the underneath of the table or placed on the chairs around the edge of the table. Divide the children into two teams and line them up at opposite ends of the table. One child in turn from each team crawls under the table to retrieve one of their cards and places it on the table. When all the cards have been collected, the children rearrange the cards to form the memory verse. Read the memory verse through several times.

Remind the children to take care when coming out from under the table.

Order under the table

Age-range: 5–9 year-olds

Gear

▶ Two sets of memory-verse cards, with one word written on each card. Each set needs to be a different colour.

▶ Table (or two tables, pushed together)

▶ Blu-tac reuseable adhesive (optional)

Hide the cards under the table—on the floor, stuck to the underneath of the table or placed on the chairs around the edge of the table. Divide the children into two teams and line them up at opposite ends of the table. One child in turn from each team crawls under the table to retrieve one of their cards and places it on the table. The children must find the words in the order that they appear in the memory verse. When all the cards have been collected, read the memory verse through several times.

Remind the children to take care when coming out from under the table.

Down the line

Age-range: 5–9 year-olds

Gear

▶ One set of memory-verse cards per team, with one word written on each card. Each set needs to be a different colour.

Divide the children into teams and seat each team, one behind another, in a line. Place a set of memory-verse cards at the front of each line. The aim of the game is to pass the memory-verse cards along the team as quickly as possible and reassemble the memory verse at the other end.

The person at the beginning of the line passes one card at a time to the next person to pass on down the line. Several cards can travel down the line at a time; however, each member of the team may only hold one card at a time. When all the cards have reached the end of the line, all the children can help to rearrange the cards into the correct order.

Obstacle

Age-range: 5–11 year-olds

Gear

- Two sets of memory-verse cards, with one word written on each card. Each set needs to be a different colour.
- Tables, chairs, hoops, etc to form an obstacle course

Prepare an obstacle course, using tables, chairs, hoops etc to crawl under, over or through. Place the memory-verse cards along the length of the obstacle course. Divide the children into two teams. One child in turn from each team travels along the obstacle course collecting one card from the memory verse and bringing it back to their team. When all the cards have been collected, the children arrange the memory verse into the correct order.

When playing this game with a mixed age group including younger children, number the cards to help the children to order the words. At the end, read through the memory verse together two or three times.

Obstacle order

Age-range: 6–11 year-olds

Gear

- Two sets of memory-verse cards, with one word written on each card. Each set needs to be a different colour.
- Tables, chairs, hoops, etc to form an obstacle course

Prepare an obstacle course, using tables, chairs, hoops, etc to crawl under, over or through. Place the memory-verse cards along the length of the obstacle course. Divide the children into two teams. One child in turn from each team travels along the obstacle course collecting one card from the memory verse and bringing it back to their team. The children are to find the words of the memory verse in order, requiring careful searching along the course. The children are not allowed to go back along the course. If they arrive at the end of the course without finding the next word in the sequence, they either have to travel the course again or the next child in the team tries to find the word. Read the memory verse together two or three times at the end.

Piggy back

Age-range: 9–11 year-olds

Gear

- One set of memory-verse cards per team, with one word written on each card. Each set needs to be a different colour.
- Blu-tac reuseable adhesive

Stick the memory-verse cards to a wall at one end of the room so that all the cards from all the teams are mixed together. Divide the children into teams. Children from each team take it in turns to piggy back a team-mate across the room to collect a card. When all the cards have been collected, the children rearrange them to show the memory verse. At the end, read through the memory verse together two or three times.

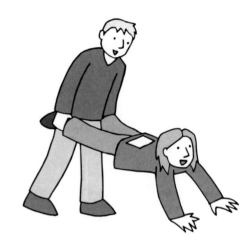

Wheelbarrow relay

Age-range: 9–11 year-olds

Gear

- One set of memory-verse cards per team, with one word written on each card. Each set needs to be a different colour.

Fold over the corners of the memory-verse cards and arrange them on the floor at one end of the room so that one corner of each card sticks up. Divide the children into teams and line them up at opposite ends of the room. Children in each team take it in turns to "wheel" a team-mate to the opposite end of the room—that is, one person walks on their hands while supported by a friend holding their legs. The "wheel barrow" picks up one of their team's cards in their teeth and is wheeled back to their team. Rearrange the cards to make the memory verse. Read through the memory verse a few times.

On the cards—Extras

The following games from "By the board" can also be played using word cards:

- **Voices** (page 10)

- **Squeak piggy squeak** (page 10)

- **Around the circle** (page 10)

- **Sign** (page 10)

- **Grandmother's footsteps** (page 10)

- **Clap** (page 11)

- **Clapman** (page 11)

- **Alphabet clap** (page 11)

- **Number clap** (page 12)

- **Bus-stop** (page 12)

- **Ladders** (page 13)

- **Gold, silver, bronze** (page 13)

SOMETHING EXTRA

Notes for leaders

All the games in this section require the use of either a board or memory-verse cards, along with something extra, such as a glove puppet or a ball. If you are using memory-verse cards, write one word of the verse on each card.

The resources you need are listed under **Gear** for each activity.

These commandments that I give you today are to be upon your hearts. Deuteronomy 6 v 6 (NIV)

Something extra—contents

Silly puppet

Age-range: 3–5 year-olds

Gear

▶ Either a set of memory-verse cards, or a black or white board
▶ A squeaking glove puppet

Display the memory verse on the board or cards and read it together several times. Introduce the children to the glove puppet. Tell the children that he is younger than them and hasn't quite learned to read or remember the memory verse yet. The puppet is going to say the memory verse out loud and they are to listen carefully to check that he gets it right. The children are to shout out when he makes a mistake and they are to tell him the correct version.

Make the glove puppet read the memory verse four or five times incorrectly before reading the memory verse together correctly.

Musical bumps

Age-range: 3–6 year-olds

Gear

▶ Either a set of memory-verse cards, or a black or white board
▶ CD, tape or MP3 player, with suitable music for your group

Write the memory verse on the board or cards. Ask the children to find a space in the room. When the music plays, the children dance or move around. As soon as the music stops, the children sit down as quickly as possible. The last child to sit down recites the memory verse. Continue playing until all the children have had a chance to recite the memory verse at least once. You may choose to remove words from the memory verse as the game progresses.

Musical statues

Age-range: 3–6 year-olds

Gear

▶ Either a set of memory-verse cards, or a black or white board
▶ CD, tape or MP3 player, with suitable music for your group

Write the memory verse on the board or cards. Divide the children into teams and ask them to find a space in the room. When the music plays, the children dance or move around. As soon as the music stops, the children freeze in a statue. The child who makes the best statue recites the memory verse and, if this is done correctly, they gain a point for their team. Any child who is seen moving after the music stops loses a point for their team unless they recite the memory verse correctly. You may choose to remove words from the memory verse as the game progresses.

Wash day

Age-range: 3–6 year-olds

Gear

▶ A set of memory-verse cards, with one word written on each card
▶ Washing line or string
▶ Pegs or paperclips to hang "washing"

Hang a washing line along one wall (or ask two helpers to be line posts!). Take care to hang the washing line where the children cannot run into it. Mix up the memory-verse cards and give them out to the children. The child with the first word comes and pegs it to the left-hand end of the washing line, followed by the child with the second word. Continue until the whole memory verse is displayed. Redistribute the cards and challenge the children to hang out the cards much quicker the second time through.

See **Hang out the washing** (page 25) for a more challenging version of this game.

If you have time, cut out card / card stock in the shape of clothes hanging on a line. Laminate the card, or cover with sticky-backed plastic, and use again and again with a dry-wipe pen.

There are some simple clothes shapes on page 30 to copy or photocopy. You can also download these pictures—see page 7 for details.

Windy wash day

Age-range: 3–6 year-olds

Gear

- A set of memory-verse cards, with one word written on each card
- Washing line or string
- Pegs or paperclips to hang "washing"

Ask two helpers to hold the washing line. Take care to hang the washing line where the children cannot run into it. Start with the word cards pegged in order on the washing line. Read the memory verse together two or three times. Tell the children it is getting windy, (the helpers shake the washing line to prove this!) and the washing will blow away. Ask one of the children to choose a word card to blow away; they unpeg this and take it back to their place. Read through the memory verse together (hold the line still) before it gets even windier and another piece of washing is chosen to blow away.

Name game

Age-range: 3–9 year-olds

Gear

- Either a set of memory-verse cards, or a black or white board
- Large ball
- Blu-tac reuseable adhesive (if using memory-verse cards)

Display the memory verse on a board or by attaching memory-verse cards to a wall. Stand all the children in a circle, with an adult in the centre holding the ball. The adult calls out the name of a child and bounces the ball at the same time. The child whose name has been called runs forward to catch the ball. If they are successful, they read or recite the memory verse. Repeat until all the children have had at least one turn. You may choose to rub out or remove words from the memory verse as the game progresses.

Hang out the washing

Age-range: 5–9 year-olds

Gear

- A set of memory-verse cards, with one word written on each card
- Washing line or string
- Pegs or paperclips to hang "washing"

Hang a washing line along one wall (or ask two helpers to be line posts). Take care to hang the washing line where the children cannot run into it. Mix up the memory-verse cards and give them out to the children. Choose one child to bring one of their cards to peg on the line. The child has to estimate the correct place to hang the card. Continue choosing children to hang up their cards until all the memory verse is displayed. The aim of the game is to hang all the cards to display the verse in order without having to move any of the cards that have already been positioned.

Hang-out-the-washing relay

Age-range: 5–9 year-olds

Gear

- A set of memory-verse cards per team, with one word written on each card
- Washing line or string
- Pegs or paperclips to hang "washing"

Hang a washing line along one wall (or ask two helpers to be line posts). Take care to hang the washing line where the children cannot run into it. Divide the children into teams and line them up at the far side of the room. Provide each team with a set of memory-verse cards and pegs. One child in turn from each team takes one card and pegs it to the washing line. The team that hangs out the washing in the correct order first wins.

Wash-day relay

Age-range: 5–9 year-olds

Gear

- A set of memory-verse cards per team, with one word written on each card
- Washing line or string
- Pegs or paperclips to hang "washing"

Hang a washing line along one wall (or ask two helpers to be line posts). Make one set of memory-verse cards for each team. Mix these up and peg to the washing line. Divide the children into teams and line them up at the opposite side of the room. One child in turn from each team races to collect one card for their team. When all the cards have been collected, the children rearrange them to make the memory verse.

As an alternative to running to collect the cards, the children can hop, jump or use their hands and feet to travel across the room.

Numbers

Age-range: 5–11 year-olds

Gear

- A set of memory-verse cards, with one word written on each card
- Large, soft ball

Divide the children into two teams, lining them up in two parallel lines about two metres apart. Number the children in each team, starting at opposite ends of the teams so that children with the same number are not opposite each other. The adult stands in-between the teams about halfway along the line.

The adult shouts out a number, bouncing the ball at the same time. The children with that number race to catch the ball. The successful child recites the memory verse and, if this is done correctly, they gain a point for their team. You may choose to display the memory verse for the children to read, removing a word each time that it is recited correctly.

Catch the stick

Age-range: 5–11 year-olds

Gear

- Either a set of memory-verse cards, or a black or white board
- A stick—for example a walking stick, or the tube from the inside of a roll of wrapping paper

Divide the children into teams and number each member of each team. Stand the teams in a large circle around an adult, who holds the stick vertically, one end resting on the floor. The adult shouts out a number, letting the stick begin to fall at the same time. The children race to catch the stick. If they are successful, they recite the memory verse and gain a point for their team. You may decide to display the memory verse, removing or rubbing out words as the game progresses.

Dressing-up relay

Age-range: 5–11 year-olds

Gear

- A set of memory-verse cards per team, with one word written on each card. Each set needs to be written on a different colour.
- A set of dressing-up clothes per team

Arrange the memory-verse cards at one end of the room so that all the cards from all the teams are mixed together. Divide the children into equal teams and line them up one behind the other at the opposite side of the room. Provide each team with a similar set of dressing-up clothes; for example: hat, scarf and gloves.

One child in turn from each team puts on the dressing-up clothes, runs to collect one card for their team, then passes their clothes to the next person in the team. When all the cards have been collected, the teams rearrange them into the correct order. Read through the memory verse together once or twice.

Newspaper game

Age-range: 6–11 year-olds

Gear

- Either a set of memory-verse cards, or a black or white board
- Newspapers
- Plain paper
- Scissors
- Glue

Display the memory verse on a board or cards. Divide the children into teams. Give each team some newspaper, scissors, glue and plain paper. The aim of the game is to make the memory verse using words and letters from the newspaper. The children in each team work together to cut and paste words from the newspaper to make the memory verse, including the reference.

For older children, make this activity more challenging by not displaying the memory verse beforehand.

Memory game

Age-range: 6–11 year-olds

Gear

- One set of memory-verse cards per team, written as described below

Make one set of memory-verse cards per team, each team's cards **written** in a different colour but on the **same** coloured card / card stock. For example, if you have two teams, team A might have the memory verse written in *red pen on yellow cards*, and team B have it written in *blue pen, but still on yellow cards*.

Seat the children in their teams around a table. Mix all the cards together and place them face down in a grid pattern on the table. The aim of the game is to find the memory verse in the correct order by turning over one card at a time. The first person in the first team turns over one card. If it is the first word of their memory verse (ie: it's the first word *and* it's written in their colour), they keep the card and have another turn; if not, they turn it back face down and the first

person in the second team has a turn. Teams and the children within the teams continue to take turns to turn over cards until all the words have been found in order. Children within the teams can remind each other where the correct card is.

Straw relay

Age-range: 6–11 year-olds

Gear

- One set of words per team, photocopied onto coloured A4 / US letter paper (to make lighter memory verse "cards" that can be lifted with a straw)
- Straws

Photocopy the memory verse onto paper and cut into individual words. Make one set per team, each set of words on a different colour. Arrange the pieces of paper on a table at one end of the room. Divide the children into teams and line them up at the opposite end of the room. Provide each child with a straw. The children in each team take turns to race across the room, suck up one word of the memory verse with their straw and bring it back to their team. If they drop their word, they suck it up again from where it fell. When all the words have been collected, rearrange to show the memory verse in order.

Be careful that the children do not run with the straw in their mouth. They should hold the straw in their hand as they race to the table, but then walk back (while sucking on the straw to keep hold of the paper).

Straw order

Age-range: 6–11 year-olds

Gear

▶ One set of words per team, photocopied onto coloured A4 / US letter paper (to make lighter memory verse "cards" that can be lifted with a straw)

▶ Straws

Photocopy the memory verse onto paper and cut into individual words. Make one set per team, with each team's memory verse on a different colour. Arrange the pieces of paper on a table at one end of the room. Divide the children into teams and line them up at the opposite end of the room. Provide each child with a straw. The children in each team take turns to race across the room, suck up one word of the memory verse with their straw and bring it back to their team. If they drop their word, they suck it up again from where it fell. The words must be collected in the order they appear in the memory verse. Read through the memory verse together when all the words have been collected and displayed in order.

Be careful that the children do not run with the straw in their mouth. They should hold the straw in their hand as they race to the table, but then walk back (while sucking on the straw to keep hold of the paper).

Tear away

Age-range: 6–11 year-olds

Gear

▶ A large piece of paper

▶ Coloured marker pens

▶ Blu-tac reuseable adhesive, drawing pins or sticky tape

Write out the memory verse on a large piece of paper, using a different colour of pen to highlight key words and the reference. Stick the paper firmly to the wall or board. Recite the memory verse together two or three times before choosing someone to tear a word out of the paper.

For older children, a forfeit could be given to anyone who tears out more than one word or causes parts of the paper to flop over. Possible forfeits could be: reciting the whole memory verse without help, reciting the previous memory verse or singing "Happy birthday".

Team tear away

Age-range: 6–11 year-olds

Gear

▶ A large piece of paper per team

▶ Coloured marker pens

▶ Blu-tac reuseable adhesive, drawing pins or sticky tape

Write out the memory verse on a large piece of paper for each team, using a different colour of pen to highlight key words and the reference. The teams take it in turns to nominate one member of their team to tear out one word from their paper and then recite the memory verse. If this is done correctly, the team gains a point. A point is deducted from the team if anyone tears out more than one word or causes parts of the paper to flop over.

For older children, a forfeit could also be given, such as reciting the whole memory verse without help, reciting a previous memory verse, singing "Happy Birthday", etc.

Tear-away jigsaw

Age-range: 6–11 year-olds

Gear

▶ The pieces from the game **Team tear away**

▶ Sticky tape

▶ Scissors

After a game of "Team tear away," the teams can be challenged to reassemble the memory verse. The team to achieve this first wins. Read through the memory verse together several times.

Something extra

Dribble dribble

Age-range: 7–11 year-olds

Gear

▶ A set of memory-verse cards per team, with one word written on each card

▶ A soft football per team

Make one set of cards per team and place at one end of the room. Divide the children into teams and line them up at the other end of the room. Set out a line of chairs along the length of the course between each team and the cards. Provide each team with a soft football. The children in each team take it in turns to dribble the football in and out of the chairs, collect one card for their team and dribble back again. The winning team is the first to collect all their cards and arrange them in the correct order.

© The Good Book Company 2008
The purchaser of *Remember Remember* is entitled to photocopy this page for use with his or her group.

SHAPE UP

Notes for leaders

The games in this section are all suitable for younger children, aged 3–7 years old. Some of these children will not yet be able to read, but they can still take part in these memory-verse activities by matching shapes. All of these games require a shape baseboard and a set of shapes per team, which can be made as follows:

Enlarge the **Shape baseboard photocopiable** (page 35) to A3 / US ledger size. Make enough copies onto A3 / US ledger card / card stock for each team to have one shape baseboard. Laminate or cover with sticky-backed plastic.

Enlarge the **Shapes photocopiable** (page 36) onto A3 / US ledger paper and write out the memory verse and reference so that one word or short phrase is on each shape. Photocopy these onto coloured card / card stock, one colour per team, and cut out so that each team has a set of shapes.

You can also download these photocopiables—see page 7 for details.

At the end of each game, read through the memory verse together three or four times.

Your word, O Lord, is eternal; it stands firm in the heavens.
Psalm 119 v 89 (NIV)

Shape up—contents

Shape hunt

Age-range: 3–7 year-olds

Gear

▶ A shape baseboard and set of shapes per team (see page 31)

Hide the shape cards around the room. Vary the difficulty of the hiding places according to the age of the children. Divide the children into teams, giving each team a baseboard. The children in each team take turns to find one shape and bring it back to their team, matching it to the board. The team who finds and matches all their shapes first wins the game.

At the end of the game, read through the memory verse together three or four times.

Shape obstacle

Age-range: 3–7 year-olds

Gear

▶ A shape baseboard and set of shapes per team (see page 31)

Prepare an obstacle course—for example, using chairs or tables to crawl under. Hide the shape cards along the obstacle course. Divide the children into teams, giving each team a baseboard. Children in each team take turns to travel along the obstacle course, collect one shape, bring it back to the team and match it to the baseboard. The winning team is the first to match all their shapes correctly.

At the end of the game, read through the memory verse together three or four times.

Shape order

Age-range: 3–7 year-olds

Gear

▶ A shape baseboard and set of shapes per team (see page 31)

Distribute the shapes around the room, so that they are fairly easy to find. Divide the children into teams and give each team a baseboard. The children take turns to find one shape at a time, with the first child hunting for the first shape on the board, the second child the next shape and so on. Continue until all the shapes have been found in the correct order. Groups may need overseeing to check that the children find the shapes in order. Any shapes that are not found in order may be re-hidden.

At the end of the game, read through the memory verse together three or four times.

Shape relay

Age-range: 3–7 year-olds

Gear

▶ A shape baseboard and set of shapes per team (see page 31)
▶ Blu-tac reuseable adhesive (if sticking shapes to board/wall)

Mix all the shapes together and stick the shape cards to a board or wall. Alternatively, arrange them on the floor or tables at one end of the room. Divide the children into equal teams, giving each team a baseboard. Line the children up in their teams at the opposite side of the room. One child in turn from each team runs to collect one shape for their team, bringing it back to a table or floor and matching it to the baseboard. The winning team is the first to have matched all their shapes.

At the end of the game, read through the memory verse together three or four times.

As an alternative to running to collect the card, the children can hop, jump or use their hands and feet to travel across the room.

REMEMBER REMEMBER

Shape-order relay

Age-range: 3–7 year-olds

Gear

- A shape baseboard and set of shapes per team (see page 31)
- Blu-tac reuseable adhesive (if sticking shapes to board/wall)

Introduce this game when the children are familiar with the **Shape relay** game (page 32). Mix all the shapes together and arrange the shapes at one end of the room. Divide the children into equal teams, giving each team a baseboard. Line the children up in their teams at the opposite side of the room. One child in turn from each team runs to collect one shape for their team, bringing it back to a table or floor and matching it to the baseboard. In this game, however, cards must be collected in the same order as shown on the baseboard. The winning team is the first to match all their shapes.

At the end of the game, read through the memory verse together three or four times.

As an alternative to running to collect the shapes, the children could hop, jump or use their hands and feet to travel across the room.

Shape balance

Age-range: 3–7 year-olds

Gear

- A shape baseboard and set of shapes per team (see page 31)
- String

Arrange the shapes on the floor or tables at one end of the room, mixing all the shapes together. Divide the children into equal teams and line them up at the opposite end of the room. Give each team a baseboard. Lay out a piece of string in front of each team, leading to the shapes at the opposite end of the room. One child in turn from each team balances along the string, collects one shape, then balances back along the string and matches the shape to the baseboard. The winning team is the first to match all their shapes to the baseboard.

At the end of the game, read through the memory verse together three or four times.

Shape dress-up

Age-range: 3–7 year-olds

Gear

- A shape baseboard and set of shapes per team (see page 31)
- A set of dressing-up clothes per team—for example: hat, scarf, gloves and coat. Ensure that each team has an equivalent set of clothes.

Arrange the shapes on the floor or tables at one end of the room. Divide the children into equal teams and line them up at the other end of the room. Give each team a baseboard and a set of dressing-up clothes. Children within each team take turns to put on the dressing-up clothes, run to collect one shape for their team, then pass on their clothes to the next person. The winning team is the first to match all their shapes to the baseboard.

At the end of the game, read through the memory verse together three or four times.

Shapes under a box

Age-range: 3–7 year-olds

Gear

- A shape baseboard and set of shapes per team (see page 31)
- A variety of junk boxes—for example, ice cream boxes or margarine tubs.

Hide the shapes under boxes at one end of the room, putting two or three shapes under each box. Divide the children into teams and line them up at the opposite end of the room. Provide each team with a baseboard. Children from each team take it in turns to run to the boxes and look under one box at a time until they find one of their shapes. Children replace the boxes each time to cover any remaining shapes. The winning team is the first to find all their shapes.

At the end of the game, read through the memory verse together three or four times.

Pushchair relay

Age-range: 3–7 year-olds

Gear

▶ A shape baseboard and set of shapes per team (see page 31)
▶ Toy pushchairs, trolleys or ride along toys

Arrange the shapes at one end of the room. Divide the children into teams and provide each team with a toy pushchair and a baseboard. Set out three chairs along the length of the course, between each team and the shapes. Children in each team take turns to wheel the pushchair in and out of the chairs to collect one shape at a time for their team. Continue taking turns until all the shapes have been collected and matched to the baseboard.

At the end of the game, read through the memory verse together three or four times.

PIECE BY PIECE

Notes for leaders

The games in this section are based on jigsaws—either picture jigsaws or line jigsaws. In both cases the children need to reassemble the jigsaw to discover the memory verse.

Instructions for making picture jigsaws are given on page 38. Line jigsaws are based on the photocopiables on pages 41–42. Details of how to make them can be found on page 39.

You can also download these photocopiables—see page 7 for details.

After the jigsaws have been assembled, read through the memory verse together three or four times.

They received the message with great eagerness and examined the Scriptures every day to see if what Paul said was true.
Acts 17 v 11 (NIV)

Piece by piece—contents

Part one—Picture jigsaws

Prepare a jigsaw for each team. Jigsaws can be a simple shape or picture with the memory verse written on or around the shape or picture (see right for examples). Each jigsaw should be photocopied or mounted onto a different colour of card / card stock so that the back of each jigsaw is a different colour. Cut each jigsaw into the same number of pieces.

Picture jigsaw

Age-range: 3–9 year-olds

Gear

▶ One set of picture jigsaw pieces per team

Hide the pieces of the jigsaw around the room face down so that each team can collect their own jigsaw. Vary the difficulty of the hiding places according to the age of the children. Divide the children into teams and allocate one colour to each team. The children take it in turns in their team to find one piece of jigsaw and bring it back to their team. Alternatively all the children from each team can hunt at the same time, finding one piece at a time and bringing it back to their team before finding another piece. It is helpful if the children and helpers know how many pieces they need to find. Once all the pieces are collected, the children rearrange them to make a picture. Read through the memory verse together three or four times at the end.

You may choose to continue reading through the memory verse, taking away one piece of jigsaw at a time until all pieces are removed and the children are reciting the verse from memory.

Picture obstacle

Age-range: 3–9 year-olds

Gear

▶ One set of picture jigsaw pieces per team

Prepare an obstacle course—for example, using chairs or tables to crawl under. Hide the jigsaw pieces face down around the obstacle course. Divide the children into two teams. Children in each team take turns to travel along the obstacle course and collect one piece of jigsaw. The winning team is the first team to assemble their jigsaw.

Read through the memory verse together three or four times at the end.

Picture relay

Age-range: 3–9 year-olds

Gear

▶ One set of picture jigsaw pieces per team

Arrange the jigsaw pieces face down at one end of the room, either on the floor or tables. Line the children up in teams at the other end of the room. Children from each team take turns to run and collect one piece of jigsaw and bring it back to their team. The winning team is the first to assemble their jigsaw.

Read through the memory verse together three or four times at the end.

As an alternative to running to collect the card, the children can hop, jump or use their hands and feet to travel across the room.

② Part two—Line jigsaws

Photocopy the jigsaw masters on pages 41–42. You can also download these photocopiables—see page 7 for details.

Write one or two words of the memory verse onto each section; then photocopy onto coloured card / card stock. Prepare one set of cards per team, each set on a different colour of card / card stock. Alternatively, cut a long strip of card / card stock into sections using a different pattern each time:

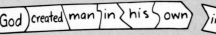

God) created \ man) in (his) own) image

Jigsaw game

Age-range: 3–9 year-olds

Gear
▶ One set of line jigsaw pieces per team

Hide the jigsaw pieces around the room, varying the difficulty of the hiding places according to the age of the children. Divide the children into teams and allocate one colour to each team. The children take turns in their team to find one piece of jigsaw and bring it back to their team. When all the pieces have been found, the children assemble their jigsaw.

After the jigsaw has been assembled, read through the memory verse three or four times together.

Jigsaw obstacles

Age-range: 3–9 year-olds

Gear
▶ One set of line jigsaw pieces per team

Prepare an obstacle course—for example, by using chairs or tables to crawl under. Hide the jigsaw pieces around the obstacle course. Divide the children into two teams. Children in each team take turns to travel along the obstacle course and collect one piece of jigsaw. The winning team is the first team to assemble their jigsaw.

After the jigsaw has been assembled, read through the memory verse three or four times together.

Jigsaw relay

Age-range: 3–9 year-olds

Gear
▶ One set of line jigsaw pieces per team

Arrange the jigsaw pieces face down at one end of the room, either on the floor or tables. Line the children up in teams at the other end of the room. Children from each team take turns to run and collect one piece of jigsaw and bring it back to their team. The winning team is the first to assemble their jigsaw.

After the jigsaw has been assembled, read through the memory verse three or four times together.

As an alternative to running to collect the jigsaw pieces, the children could hop or jump along the course.

Hidden jigsaws

Age-range: 3–9 year-olds

Gear

- ▶ One set of line jigsaw pieces per team
- ▶ Boxes, tubs etc to cover jigsaw pieces

Mix up the jigsaw pieces and place these on the floor at one end of the room. Cover each piece of jigsaw with a box; for example, an old margarine tub. Alternatively, use a piece of card / card stock to cover the jigsaws. Divide the children into colour teams. The children take turns to jump across the room and look under one box. If the piece of jigsaw underneath belongs to their team, they collect it; if not, they return to their team and the next person tries to find a piece of jigsaw.

After the jigsaw has been assembled, read through the memory verse three or four times together.

Hidden jigsaw challenge

Age-range: 5–9 year-olds

Gear

- ▶ One set of line jigsaw pieces per team
- ▶ Boxes, tubs etc to cover jigsaw pieces

Mix up the jigsaw pieces and place these on the floor at one end of the room. Cover each piece of jigsaw with a box; for example, a margarine tub, or piece of card / card stock. Divide the children into colour teams. The aim of the game is to find the words of the memory verse in order. The children take turns to run across the room and look under one box. If the piece of jigsaw underneath is the one they need to find, they collect it; if not, they continue looking under other boxes until they find the correct piece. The winning team is the first to collect all their pieces and assemble their jigsaw.

After the jigsaw has been assembled, read through the memory verse three or four times together.

As an alternative to running to collect the jigsaw pieces, the children could hop or jump along the course.

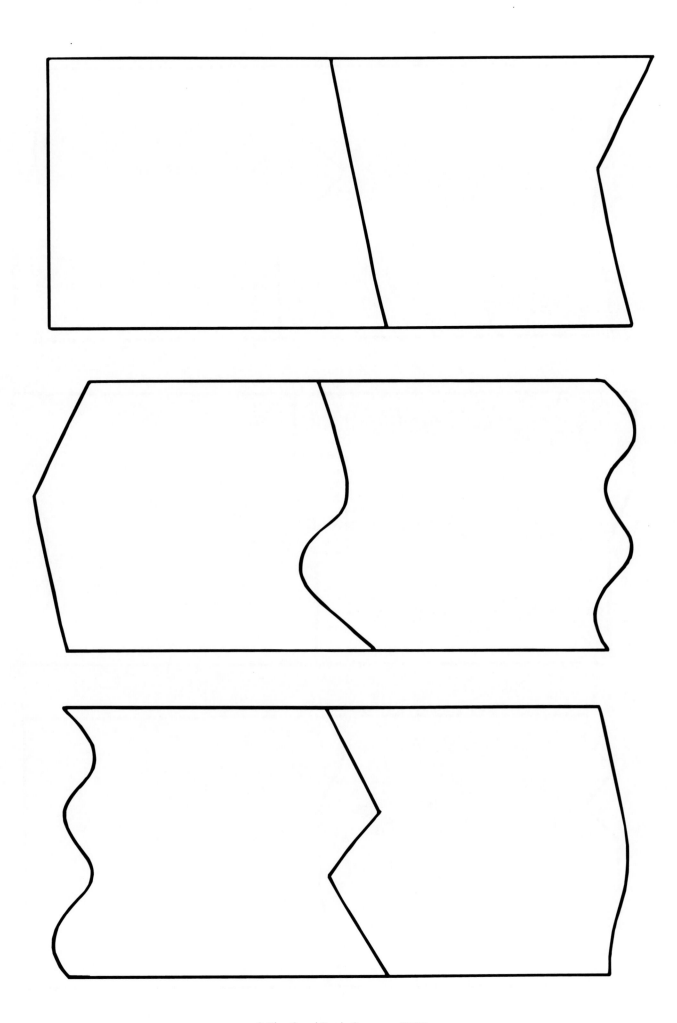

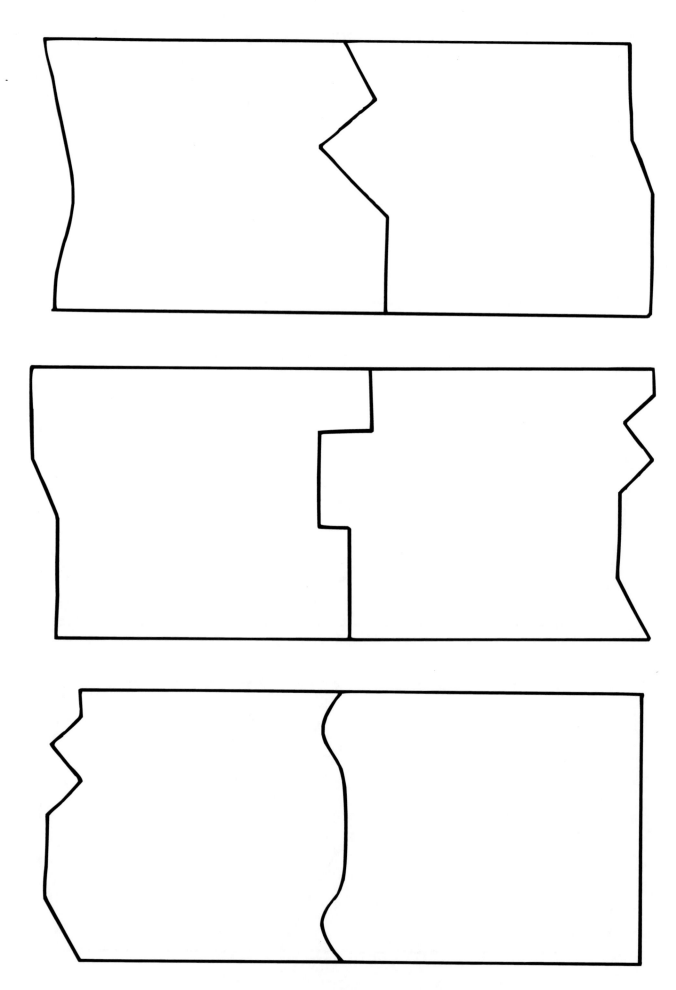

BOX CLEVER

Notes for leaders

The games in this section require a set of memory verse boxes per team, which can be made as follows:

Collect empty boxes in a variety of sizes, enough for a set of boxes for each team. Photocopy the memory verse onto card / card stock, using a different colour for each team. Cut up and attach to the boxes so that there are one or two words on each box. If you attach the words with Blu-tac reuseable adhesive, you will be able to reuse the boxes for future activities. Store the boxes stacked inside one another.

You may find it helpful, before trying any of the following activities, to read the practical tips on page 7. In particular, remember to use lower-case letters when writing out the memory verse. Unless you are teaching very young children who are not yet reading, you should include the Bible reference as well as the verse.

At the end of each game, read through the memory verse together three or four times.

The grass withers and the flowers fall, but the word of our God stands forever. Isaiah 40 v 8 (NIV)

Box clever—contents

Wall

Age-range: 5–11 year-olds

Gear

▶ One set of memory verse boxes

Ask the children to assemble one set of boxes into a wall. When assembled, read through the memory verse together once or twice. Ask a child to take away a box without knocking the wall down. Read through the memory verse again, replacing the missing words. Continue taking the boxes away and reading through the memory verse each time.

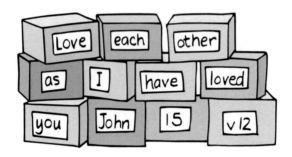

Box relay

Age-range: 5–11 year-olds

Gear

▶ One set of memory verse boxes for each team

Provide one set of memory verse boxes per team. Arrange the boxes at one end of the room so that all the teams' boxes are mixed together. The children line up in teams at the opposite end of the room, taking turns within their team to run and collect one box. The winning team is the first to assemble their memory verse as a wall or tower.

Read through the memory verse together three or four times at the end.

As an alternative to running to collect the boxes, the children can hop, jump or use their hands and feet to travel across the room.

Obstacle boxes

Age-range: 5–11 year-olds

Gear

▶ One set of memory verse boxes for each team
▶ Tables, chairs, etc to make an obstacle course

Place the boxes around an obstacle course. One child in turn from each team travels along the obstacle course collecting one box from the memory verse and bringing it back to their team. When all the boxes have been collected, the children arrange them into a wall to show the memory verse in the correct order. The winning team is the first to be seated quietly behind their wall.

Read through the memory verse together three or four times at the end.

Tottering towers

Age-range: 5–11 year-olds

Gear

▶ One set of memory verse boxes for each team

Provide one set of boxes per team. Divide the children into teams and line them up in different corners of the room. Put all the boxes face down in the centre of the room so that the team colours are hidden. One child in turn from each team races to the centre of the room and collects one box for their team. The children have to find all the boxes for their team and then assemble the boxes into a tower showing the memory verse in the correct order. The team that assembles the memory verse first wins.

Read through the memory verse together three or four times at the end.

Base up

Age-range: 7–11 year-olds

Gear

▶ One set of memory verse boxes for each team

Place the boxes face down around the room. Divide the children into teams and line them up in different corners of the room. The children in each team take turns to search for one of their team's boxes. The boxes need to be found in reverse order, starting with the reference to build the memory verse from the bottom up. The winning team is the first to have a complete tower. Any team that sabotages another team's tower is disqualified.

Read through the memory verse together three or four times at the end.

Base-up relay

Age-range: 7–11 year-olds

Gear

▶ One set of memory verse boxes for each team

Place the boxes face up at one end of the room. Divide the children into teams and line them up at the opposite end of the room. The children in each team take turns to race across the room and collect one box for their team. The boxes need to be collected in reverse order, starting with the reference. The children build their tower from the bottom up as each box is found. Any boxes that are found in the wrong order are taken back and the correct box found. The winning team is the first to assemble their boxes into a tower. Any team that sabotages another team's tower is disqualified.

Read through the memory verse together three or four times at the end.

SOMETHING MORE

Notes for leaders

All the games in this section require a little extra preparation. They would be particularly suitable for special sessions, during activities such as holiday clubs or camps, or whenever you find yourself with some extra preparation time.

The resources you need are listed under **Gear** for each activity.

Memory verse

All Scripture is God-breathed and is useful for teaching, rebuking, correcting and training in righteousness, so that the man of God may be thoroughly equipped for every good work.
2 Timothy 3 v 16–17 (NIV)

Something more—contents

Go fish

Age-range: 3–7 year-olds

Gear

▶ One magnetic fishing rod per team
▶ One set of fish per team

Write each word of the memory verse onto a paper fish; then attach a paperclip to the nose of each fish. Make one set of fish per team, each team's fish a different colour. Make one fishing rod per team by attaching a small magnet to a short rod with string.

Spread the fish out on the floor or on a piece of blue material at the one end of the room. Alternatively, put all the fish into a bucket or box decorated with a sea theme. Put the fishing rods next to the fish. The children from each team take turns to race across the room, pick up their team's fishing rod and catch one of their team's fish. If they catch another team's fish, they throw that back into the "water" and try again. When they have caught one of their fish, they take it back to their team, leaving the fishing rod next to the fish. When they have caught all the fish, they rearrange them to show the memory verse in the correct order.

Read through the memory verse together three or four times at the end.

Lost sheep

Age-range: 3–7 year-olds

Gear

▶ One card / card stock sheep for each word of the memory verse
▶ Blu-tac reuseable adhesive

Draw and cut out enough sheep to write each word of the memory verse and reference onto a sheep. (You may prefer to use the photocopiable on page 54.) If possible, prepare a background of blue and green card / card stock and blu-tac the sheep to this "field" so that the memory verse reads in the correct order. Read through the verse together several times before asking a child to remove one of the sheep. Continue reading through and removing sheep until the children are reciting the verse from memory.

As an alternative to sheep, use shapes that link to your story; for example: fish shapes, lost coins, stars or angels. There are some examples on the photocopiables on pages 55–56. You can also download these photocopiables—see page 7 for details.

Found sheep

Age-range: 3–7 year-olds

Gear

▶ One card / card stock sheep (or other shape, see **Lost sheep** above) for each word of the memory verse
▶ Blu-tac reuseable adhesive

Use the sheep or other shapes to play a finding game. Hide the shapes around the room. Divide the children into teams. Children within each team take turns to hunt for one of their shapes and bring it back to their team. When all the shapes have been found, the children rearrange them to show the memory verse.

To teach the importance of finding the one lost sheep or coin (if teaching from Luke 15), you may choose not to hide the last shape for each team. Allow all the children from all the teams to search for the shape for up to one minute before stopping the children and giving them the last shape. Don't allow the children to search too long and become frustrated.

Windows

Age-range: 3–7 year-olds

Gear

- ▶ Window card with flaps cut into it (either copy page 57 or download—see page 7 for details)
- ▶ Paper
- ▶ Blu-tac reuseable adhesive

Photocopy a window template (page 57) onto card / card stock, preferably enlarging it to A3 / US ledger. Cut round three sides of each window leaving a hinge on the outside edge of the card so that each window opens without covering any other window. Photocopy a second template onto paper and write the memory verse into the windows so that there are one or two words in each space. Attach the paper to the back of the card and open all the flaps to show the words.

Read through the memory verse together two or three times. Choose one child to come and close a window. Read through the memory verse again before choosing a different child to close another window. Repeat until the children are reciting the verse from memory. The window card may be reused for different memory verses by blu-tacking another piece of paper to the back of the card.

Feely box game

Age-range: 3–9 year-olds

Gear

- ▶ A feely box (see below)
- ▶ Two sets of memory-verse cards, each set on a different shape

Make a feely box using a medium-sized grocery box. Cut one hole in each end of the box, each large enough for the children to put their hands through. Seal the box closed and cover with wrapping paper.

Prepare two sets of memory-verse cards, making each set with a different shape of card / card stock. Put the memory-verse cards into the feely box and place the feely box on a table at one end of the room. Divide the children into two teams and line them up at the other end of the room. The children in each team take turns to race across the room to the feely box. The children put their hand in one hole to feel for a card that is the correct shape for their team. The winning team is the first to assemble the memory verse in the correct order.

Skittles

Age-range: 3–9 year-olds

Gear

- ▶ A set of memory verse skittles (see below)
- ▶ Ball

Prepare a set of skittles by folding pieces of card / card stock into three. Write the memory verse at the top of the middle section and stand on end.

Arrange the skittles in a line, so that they are well spaced and the words of the memory verse are in the correct order. Read the memory verse through several times. Choose one child to roll the ball at the skittles, so that one or two of them are knocked over. Remove these skittles from the playing area. Read through the memory verse again, filling in the missing words. Children continue to take turns at rolling the ball until all the skittles have been knocked over and removed.

Pairs

Age-range: 3–11 year-olds

Gear

▶ A set of memory-verse cards per team, each word written in a different colour and each team's words on different coloured card / card stock

▶ Coloured felt-tip pens

Write each word of the memory verse and reference onto a card, writing each word with a different coloured felt-tip. Cut each word into two so that a pair of cards makes one word. Make one set of cards per team, each team's memory verse on a different coloured card.

Hide the cards around the room, varying the difficulty of the hiding places according to the age of the children. Divide the children into teams. Children in each team take turns to find one piece of card and its matching half and bring these back to the team. When all the words have been found the children arrange them into the correct order.

To make the game more challenging for older children, write all the words in the same colour.

When playing with younger children, allow the children to find just one piece and match up the halves when all the cards have been found.

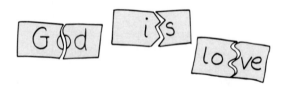

Double pairs

Age-range: 3–11 year-olds

Gear

▶ A set of memory-verse cards per team, each word written in a different colour and each team's words on different coloured card / card stock

▶ Coloured felt-tip pens

▶ Ties, as for a three-legged race (optional)

Write each word of the memory verse and reference onto a card, writing each word with a different coloured felt-tip. Cut each word into two so that a pair of cards makes one word. Make one set of cards per team, each team's memory verse on a different coloured card.

Hide the cards around the room, varying the difficulty of the hiding places according to the age of the children.

Hide the two parts of the pair close together when playing with younger children. Pair up the children: younger children may hold hands; older children may be tied together as in a three-legged race. Divide the pairs into teams.

The pairs of children in each team take turns to find a pair of cards. The children must stay linked together and find both parts of a word before returning to their team and allowing the next pair to search for a word. The winning team is the first to collect all their words and arrange them in order.

To make the game more challenging for older children, write all the words in the same colour.

Pairs around the chairs

Age-range: 3–11 year-olds

Gear

▶ A set of memory-verse cards per team, each word written in a different colour and each team's words on different coloured card / card stock

▶ Coloured felt-tip pens

▶ Ties, as for a three-legged race (optional)

▶ Chairs

Write each word of the memory verse and reference onto a card, writing each word with a different coloured felt-tip. Cut each word into two so that a pair of cards makes one word. Make one set of cards per team, each team's memory verse on a different coloured card. Place the cards on tables at one end of the room.

Pair up the children, younger children holding hands and older children tied together as in a three-legged race. Divide these pairs into teams and line the teams up at the other end of the room. Place several chairs along the length of the course, between each team and the cards. The children have to race up the room in their pairs, weaving in and out of the chairs, to collect one complete word, each child finding one half of the word. When all the cards have been collected, rearrange the words to form the memory verse. Read through the memory verse together three or four times.

Stepping stones

Age-range: 5–9 year-olds

Gear

▶ A set of stepping stones per team, each team's stones on different coloured card / card stock
▶ A "river" eg: blue material or string

Write each word of the memory verse onto a stepping stone-shaped piece of paper. Make one set of stepping stones for each team, with each team's stones in a different colour. Lay out a "river" about two thirds of the way along the room. This could be made with a piece of blue material, string or lines marked on the floor. Hide the stepping stones in the larger part of the room, varying the difficulty of the hiding places according to the age of the children.

Divide the children into teams and line them up in the larger section of the room. Explain to the children that they need to cross the river. To do this they need to find the stepping stones that are hidden this side of the river. The children in each team take turns to find a stepping-stone. When all the stones have been collected, the children place them in the river in the correct order. They are not allowed to step in the river, but they may step on stones that they have already collected and placed. When all the stones are in the river in the correct order, they walk across one at a time chanting the memory verse as they go. The winning team is the first to reach the other side of the river.

You may choose to make this more challenging for older children by asking them to find the stepping stones in order and place these in the river as they find them.

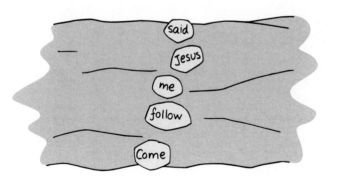

In a box

Age-range: 5–11 year-olds

Gear

▶ A set of memory-verse cards per team, each set on different coloured card / card stock
▶ Two or three large boxes
▶ Newspaper or polystyrene pieces

Fill two or three large boxes with balls of scrunched-up newspaper or polystyrene pieces. Mix up the memory-verse cards and hide some of each team's cards in each box. Place the boxes at one end of the room. Divide the children into teams and line up at the opposite end of the room. Children in each team take turns to run across the room and look in the boxes for one of their team's cards. The children rearrange the words to show the memory verse when all the cards have been found. Read through the memory verse together several times.

Order in a box

Age-range: 5–11 year-olds

Gear

▶ A set of memory-verse cards per team, each set on different coloured card / card stock
▶ Two or three large boxes
▶ Newspaper or polystyrene pieces

Fill two or three large boxes with balls of scrunched-up newspaper or polystyrene pieces. Mix up the memory-verse cards and hide some of each team's cards in each box. Place the boxes at one end of the room. Divide the children into teams and line up at the opposite end of the room. Children in each team take turns to run across the room and look in one of the boxes for one of their team's cards. The words must be found in the order in which they appear in the memory verse. Children may continue to look in the boxes until they find the correct card. Read through the memory verse together several times at the end of the game.

Stomp

Age-range: 6–11 year-olds

Gear

- ▶ Coloured balloons
- ▶ Small pieces of paper
- ▶ Rubbish bin
- ▶ Ear plugs are optional!

Write out each word or short phrase of the memory verse onto a small piece of paper. Roll these up and place them inside coloured balloons; then inflate the balloons. Use different coloured balloons for each team. Place all the balloons on the floor at one end of the room and line the children up in teams at the opposite end.

The children in each team take turns to race to the opposite end of the room, stomp on one of their team's balloons and bring the piece of paper back to their team. When all the pieces of paper have been collected, the children arrange these to show the memory verse in the correct order. Read through the memory verse several times. You may choose to take away one or two words each time you read through.

At the end of the game, challenge each team to collect the remains of their team's balloons. The winning team is the first to have put all these in the bin.

String along

Age-range: 6–11 year-olds

Gear

- ▶ A set of memory-verse cards per team, with each set on a different colour of card / card stock
- ▶ Hole-punch
- ▶ String

Create a set of memory-verse cards for each team, writing one word on each card. Use the hole-punch to make holes at either side of each card so that the cards can be strung together. Hide the memory-verse cards around the room. Divide the children into teams and give each team a long piece of string. Children in each team take turns to find the memory-verse cards in the correct order. As each card is found, it is strung onto the string until the memory verse is displayed in order.

To make this game more challenging for older children, the words could be found in reverse order.

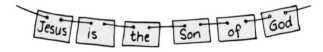

String-along relay

Age-range: 6–11 year-olds

Gear

- ▶ A set of memory-verse cards per team, with each set on a different colour of card / card stock
- ▶ Hole-punch
- ▶ String

Make a set of memory-verse cards per team, punching holes into the top corners of each card. Put the memory-verse cards at one end of the room and line up the children in teams at the other end. Give each team a long piece of string. Children in each team take turns to race across the room to collect the memory-verse cards in the order that they appear in the verse. As each card is collected, it is strung onto the string. When all the cards have been collected and the memory verse assembled in order, the children hold up the completed verse.

Link up

Age-range: 6–11 year-olds

Gear
- A set of memory-verse cards per team, with each set on a different colour of card / card stock
- Hole-punch
- Treasury tags (from a stationery shop)
- Chairs

Make a set of memory-verse cards per team. Punch holes into all four corners of each card. Hide the memory-verse cards around the room. Divide the children into teams and give each team a pile of treasury tags and a chair. The children in each team take turns to find the memory-verse cards in order, starting with the first word of the memory verse. As each card is found, the children attach it to the bottom of the previous card using the treasury tags. When all the cards have been found and linked together, one member of the team stands on the chair and holds up the memory verse.

Read through the memory verse together several times at the end.

Link-up relay

Age-range: 6–11 year-olds

Gear
- A set of memory-verse cards per team, with each set on a different colour of card / card stock
- Hole-punch
- Treasury tags
- Chairs

Make a set of memory-verse cards per team, punching holes in the corners of each card. Put the memory-verse cards at one end of the room. Line up the children, in teams, at the other end of the room. Children in each team take turns to fetch one card for their team. Cards are collected in the order that they appear in the memory verse and are linked to the previous card, using the treasury tags, as they are collected. When all the cards have been found and linked together, one member of the team stands on the chair and holds up the memory verse.

Read through the memory verse together several times at the end.

Peggy

Age-range: 6–11 year-olds

Gear
- A set of pegs per team
- String or card / card stock

Write the memory verse and reference onto pegs so that one word of the memory verse is on each peg and there is one set of pegs per team. Hide the pegs around the room. Divide the children into teams and provide each team with a piece of string or strip of card / card stock. Children in each team take turns to search for a peg to clip onto their string. The winning team is the first to assemble the memory verse in the correct order.

Read the memory verse through together several times at the end of the game.

Hat game

Age-range: 9–11 year-olds

Gear
- A set of memory-verse cards
- A hat per child, made from strips of card / card stock

Use strips of card / card stock to make enough hats for your group. Attach one or two memory-verse cards to each hat so that the memory verse can be displayed in order. Line up the children and give out the hats without the children seeing which hat they are wearing.

The aim of the game is for the children to sort themselves into memory verse order by looking at each other's hats and swapping places with one person at a time. The children are only allowed to swap places with someone standing next to them in the line. The children are not allowed to tell each other what is on their hat, but can tell each other which way to move along the line.

REMEMBER REMEMBER

tree/bush

castle/city

coin

angel

fish

star

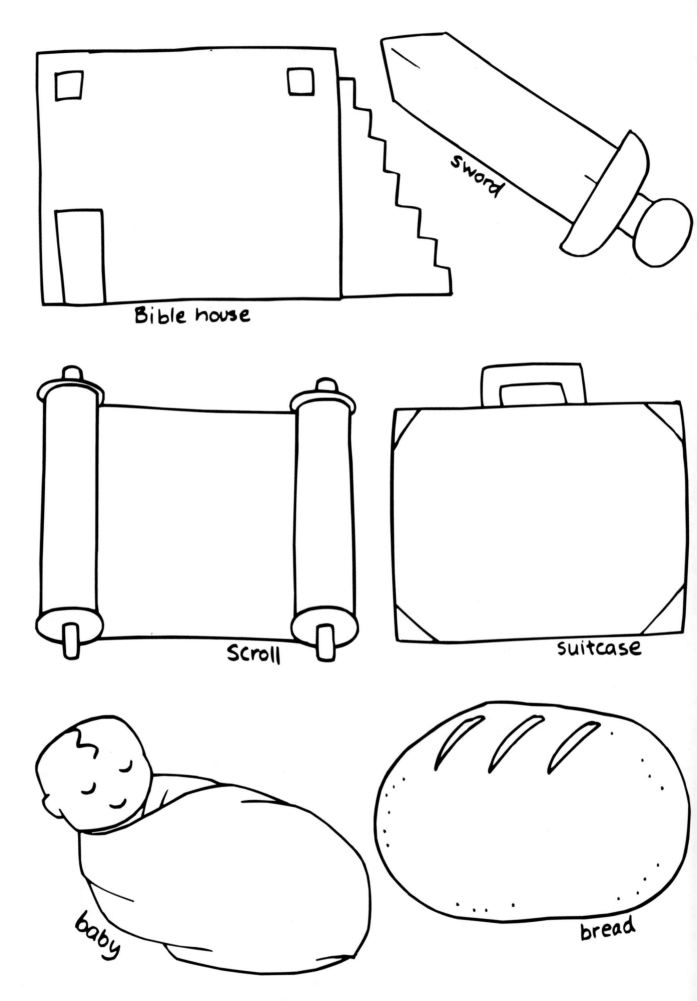

Bible house

sword

Scroll

suitcase

baby

bread

APPENDIX

MEMORY-VERSE ACTIVITIES LISTED BY AGE-RANGE

Activity					Age					Page
	3	4	5	6	7	8	9	10	11	
Silly puppet	✔	✔	✔							24
Musical bumps	✔	✔	✔	✔						24
Musical statues	✔	✔	✔	✔						24
Wash day	✔	✔	✔	✔						24
Windy wash day	✔	✔	✔	✔						25
Shape hunt	✔	✔	✔	✔	✔					32
Shape order	✔	✔	✔	✔	✔					32
Shape obstacle	✔	✔	✔	✔	✔					32
Shape relay	✔	✔	✔	✔	✔					32
Shape-order relay	✔	✔	✔	✔	✔					33
Shape balance	✔	✔	✔	✔	✔					33
Shape dress-up	✔	✔	✔	✔	✔					33
Shapes under a box	✔	✔	✔	✔	✔					33
Pushchair relay	✔	✔	✔	✔	✔					34
Go fish	✔	✔	✔	✔	✔					48
Lost sheep	✔	✔	✔	✔	✔					48
Found sheep	✔	✔	✔	✔	✔					48
Windows	✔	✔	✔	✔	✔					49
Voices	✔	✔	✔	✔	✔	✔				10
Squeak piggy squeak	✔	✔	✔	✔	✔	✔				10
Around the circle	✔	✔	✔	✔	✔	✔				10
Name game	✔	✔	✔	✔	✔	✔	✔			25
Picture jigsaw	✔	✔	✔	✔	✔	✔	✔			38
Picture obstacle	✔	✔	✔	✔	✔	✔	✔			38
Picture relay	✔	✔	✔	✔	✔	✔	✔			38
Jigsaw game	✔	✔	✔	✔	✔	✔	✔			39
Jigsaw relay	✔	✔	✔	✔	✔	✔	✔			39
Jigsaw obstacles	✔	✔	✔	✔	✔	✔	✔			39
Hidden jigsaws	✔	✔	✔	✔	✔	✔	✔			40
Hidden-jigsaw challenge			✔	✔	✔	✔	✔			40
Feely box game	✔	✔	✔	✔	✔	✔	✔			49
Skittles	✔	✔	✔	✔	✔	✔	✔			49

Activity	3	4	5	6	7	8	9	10	11	Page
Sign	✔	✔	✔	✔	✔	✔	✔	✔	✔	10
Pairs	✔	✔	✔	✔	✔	✔	✔	✔	✔	50
Double pairs	✔	✔	✔	✔	✔	✔	✔	✔	✔	50
Pairs around the chair	✔	✔	✔	✔	✔	✔	✔	✔	✔	50
Grandmother's footsteps			✔	✔	✔					10
Word sort			✔	✔	✔					16
People sort			✔	✔	✔					16
Pop-up			✔	✔	✔					16
Zig-zag			✔	✔	✔					16
Wipe-out			✔	✔	✔	✔	✔			11
All change			✔	✔	✔	✔	✔			11
Clap			✔	✔	✔	✔	✔			11
Clapman			✔	✔	✔	✔	✔			11
Alphabet clap			✔	✔	✔	✔	✔			11
Number clap			✔	✔	✔	✔	✔			12
Turn about			✔	✔	✔	✔	✔			17
Take away			✔	✔	✔	✔	✔			17
Go find			✔	✔	✔	✔	✔			18
Relay			✔	✔	✔	✔	✔			18
Relay order			✔	✔	✔	✔	✔			18
Order order			✔	✔	✔	✔	✔			19
Under the table			✔	✔	✔	✔	✔			19
Order under the table			✔	✔	✔	✔	✔			19
Down the line			✔	✔	✔	✔	✔			19
Hang out the washing			✔	✔	✔	✔	✔			25
Hang-out-the-washing relay			✔	✔	✔	✔	✔			25
Wash-day relay			✔	✔	✔	✔	✔			26
Stepping stones			✔	✔	✔	✔	✔			51
Bus stop			✔	✔	✔	✔	✔	✔	✔	12
Hangman			✔	✔	✔	✔	✔	✔	✔	12
Ladders			✔	✔	✔	✔	✔	✔	✔	13
Obstacle			✔	✔	✔	✔	✔	✔	✔	20
Numbers			✔	✔	✔	✔	✔	✔	✔	26
Catch the stick			✔	✔	✔	✔	✔	✔	✔	26
Dressing-up relay			✔	✔	✔	✔	✔	✔	✔	26
Wall			✔	✔	✔	✔	✔	✔	✔	44
Box relay			✔	✔	✔	✔	✔	✔	✔	44
Obstacle boxes			✔	✔	✔	✔	✔	✔	✔	44
Tottering towers			✔	✔	Age	✔	✔	✔	✔	44

Activity	3	4	5	6	Age 7	8	9	10	11	Page
In a box			✔	✔	✔	✔	✔	✔	✔	51
Order in a box			✔	✔	✔	✔	✔	✔	✔	51
Stomp				✔	✔	✔	✔	✔	✔	52
Chain game				✔	✔	✔	✔			17
Obstacle order				✔	✔	✔	✔	✔	✔	20
Newspaper game				✔	✔	✔	✔	✔	✔	27
Memory game				✔	✔	✔	✔	✔	✔	27
Straw relay				✔	✔	✔	✔	✔	✔	27
Straw order				✔	✔	✔	✔	✔	✔	28
Tear away				✔	✔	✔	✔	✔	✔	28
Team tear away				✔	✔	✔	✔	✔	✔	28
Tear-away jigsaw				✔	✔	✔	✔	✔	✔	28
String along				✔	✔	✔	✔	✔	✔	52
String-along relay				✔	✔	✔	✔	✔	✔	52
Link up				✔	✔	✔	✔	✔	✔	53
Link-up relay				✔	✔	✔	✔	✔	✔	53
Peggy				✔	✔	✔	✔	✔	✔	53
Gold, silver, bronze					✔	✔	✔	✔	✔	13
Circle sort					✔	✔	✔	✔	✔	17
Dribble dribble					✔	✔	✔	✔	✔	29
Base up					✔	✔	✔	✔	✔	45
Base-up relay					✔	✔	✔	✔	✔	45
Piggy back							✔	✔	✔	20
Wheelbarrow relay							✔	✔	✔	20
Hat game							✔	✔	✔	53

INDEX

MEMORY-VERSE ACTIVITIES LISTED ALPHABETICALLY

 **RESOURCES**

One Day Wonders

These books include everything you need to run Bible activity events for children and families. The flexible material provides a wide range of fun activities to choose from.

Programme options show how to use the material for a two-hour or four-hour children's event, or a one-and-a-half-hour family event. All of the activities are linked to the theme, and are built around a choice of Bible-centred talk outlines, which are supported by funsheets for small groups.

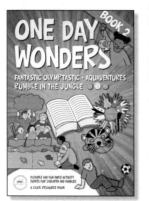

One Day Wonders contains everything you need to run a successful and memorable event: pictures, craft templates, publicity outlines and Bible funsheets can all be photocopied from the book or downloaded from any of The Good Book Company's websites.

- **One Day Wonders Book 1** contains outlines for events at Christmas, Easter and Halloween. There's a wide range of activities and ideas for Bible activity events that celebrate Christmas and Easter, and to help churches offer an alternative event at Halloween time.

- **One Day Wonders Book 2** contains everything you need to run three themed Bible activity events: Fantastic Olymptastic (a sporting theme), Aquaventures (water fun) and Rumble in the Jungle (a jungle-themed event). These events can be run at any time of year.

The above resources are available from:

UK:	www.thegoodbook.co.uk
North America:	www.thegoodbook.com
Australia:	www.thegoodbook.com.au

the good book COMPANY

CLICK teaching material

CLICK has a "biblical theology" framework, which means it teaches "little stories" as part of the "Big Story" of the Bible.

- Each unit of ten sessions is linked together (often from one book of the Bible).

- These links are reinforced by full-colour teacher's posters and child components.

- The key teaching point of a unit (this is often the key teaching point of the Bible book the unit is based on) will be reinforced each week, so that children remember and understand it.

CLICK is suitable for church groups, mid-week groups and after-school clubs. **CLICK** material will help you teach the Bible faithfully and effectively to the children in your group. It is easy to use and covers three age groups: 3-5s, 5-7s and 8-11s. The sample pack available will allow you to review the whole syllabus and see examples of the child components before you commit to using it with your group.

CLICK is only available from our UK website:
www.thegoodbook.co.uk/click

REMEMBER REMEMBER AUTHOR: ANDREA MARSHALL

Andrea trained as a primary school teacher and has been teaching the Bible to children for over 20 years. She lives in Coventry with her husband and daughter and attends Canley Evangelical Church. *Remember Remember* is her first book for The Good Book Company.

SERIES EDITOR: ALISON MITCHELL

Alison is the children's editor at The Good Book Company, where she has written a range of Bible-reading notes for children and families, as well as editing CLICK teaching material. Alison is also involved with training events around the country for children's and youth leaders.